RISE

mini mindful morning meditations

to awaken your mind and body to a
refreshing
relaxing
transformational
fresh start

JULIE SKON

RISE

Copyright © 2022 by Julie Skon

IBSN (hardcover) 979-8-9852794-4-3
ISBN (paperback) 979-8-9852794-2-9
ISBN (ebook) 979-8-9852794-5-0

To my daughters,

Thank you for laughing with me
during the chaotic mornings
and embracing the peaceful ones.
You make every morning special.
I am so GRATEFUL for you!

I love you,
Mom

Today might just be the most
beautiful day of your life.
And, the best part?
You have everything within
you to make it so.

— Julie Skon

CONTENTS

A NOTE FROM THE AUTHOR

Hello, I am so happy and grateful that you found your way to RISE! I wrote the meditations included in this book over many calm, stress-free, and beautiful mornings. I emphasize these words because in the past, "calm", "stress-free", and "beautiful" would not be how I typically described my mornings. "Beautiful" maybe, but more along the lines of "beautiful chaos."

Just a few years ago, I was one of the millions of people tumbling out of bed in the morning to the sound of my blaring alarm clock, racing to check my phone or send an email, hustling to get my kids to school on time, struggling with stress-induced illnesses, and I was feeling overwhelmingly disconnected, exhausted, and burnt out. Basically, my days felt completely out of my control and I reached a point where I knew something needed to change, quickly. I enrolled in a 6-week meditation teacher certification course with Unplug and Davidji and it is where I discovered the magic of meditation. Now, I am not one to meditate for hours daily, but developing a practice of mini morning meditations has changed my life on so many levels. Just a few minutes of mindful meditation in the morning has led me to be more consciously present in the special moments of the day, I take deeper breaths as stress arises within me, I have greater mindset clarity, I feel grounded and happier, and my body has even healed.

I believe that meditation has a way of finding you when you need it the most. Maybe you are one of the lucky ones who have already experienced the benefits of morning meditation. And, if so, I hope that you explore these meditations and experience an even deeper connection with yourself and with your morning. And, if you are new to morning meditation, WELCOME! I invite you to dive into these pages and *take back your mornings*. Use these meditations to start your day, to refresh your mind and body as you wake, and to mindfully RISE in the morning ready and relaxed for an extraordinary day ahead.

RISE

*Tips to get the most out of this book
and your morning meditations*

WHO

Tip: Keep it simple. The only element that you need for meditation to work its magic, is YOU.

You, and a willingness to slow down and connect to your mind and body, even if just for just a few moments a day. Meditation is simple and pure – it is just YOU connecting to YOU.

WHAT

Tip: Meditation is a practice of being open and curious to your thoughts, feelings, emotions, and sensations that you are experiencing in the moment, without judgment.

There are many misconceptions about what meditation is and is not. One big misunderstanding is that meditation is about learning how to stop your thoughts. Well, this is impossible and leads to frustration for almost anyone that tries it. Meditation is not about stopping one of the 60k+ thoughts you have every day. Instead, it is a practice of witnessing what comes up for you in your mind, body, heart, and soul, judgment-free, and then letting it go by returning your focus to your breath. So, if you are in meditation and you find your thoughts wandering to your grocery list, ruminating over the argument you had, or holding onto the stress you are carrying - simply witness what is coming up for you and gently let it go by returning your attention to your inhales and exhales, allowing yourself to just be.

WHEN

Tip: If you allow meditation to be the gentle start to your morning, you will create a mindful ripple effect that touches you throughout your day.

First things, first. The sooner you get your morning meditation in, the faster it gets to work its benefits on your mind and body. The important element here is that it is a special, quiet time for you. If it helps, set your alarm ten minutes earlier than you normally would and allow some quiet time to be all yours.

WHERE

Tip: Wherever you choose to meditate, make it your space, a place that you love, somewhere that you look forward to being within and is comfortable and easy to access.

I love a good "beditation" in the morning – tapping in before energy has been poured into anything else. Before you rise and shine, read through your meditation for the day and just stay in your peaceful place. Ignore your phone or anything else, prop up a pillow if you think you will fall back asleep, and dive right in.

I also love to create a sacred space within my home for meditation. It does not have to be fancy and filled with crystals, aromatherapy, and meaningful items *although of course it can be*. However you like it, the importance of a sacred space is that it is *your* space. It can be at a table, on the floor, your favorite chair, or anywhere in your home that you love to be. When you wake up, go to that space, get cozy, take a few deep breaths and sink right into the moment.

WHY

Tip: Pay attention to how morning meditations affect you throughout the day, be aware of deeper breaths you take, increased pauses between thoughts and actions, and celebrate the awareness of being more mindfully present.

There are more and more scientific studies proving the benefits of meditation. To name just a few, meditation has been shown to reduce stress, lower heart rate, improve sleep, increase feelings of happiness, elevate mood, create mindset clarity, improve decision making, deepen connections with ourselves and others, and it even shrinks our amygdalas (our brain's center that manages fight or flight processing) and *so much more.*

I like to say the old saying that "the proof is in the pudding." Because, at the end of the day, this meditation experience is about how it affects YOU. Check-in with yourself. How do you feel before, during, and after you meditate?

HOW

Tip: Use these meditation to serve you by allowing your intuition to guide you to which meditation to practice that morning.

This book is designed for you to flip to any meditation that calls to you. You can of course challenge yourself to do one at a time, from beginning to end, but feel no pressure to do so. Each meditation is designed to be about 3-5 minutes in length, but the time spent on each is entirely up to you. If you are reading the text, read through the meditation a few times to allow the practice to sink in. Close your eyes for the times when you are reflecting on a question, or repeating a mantra - remember there is no judgment or "right" or "wrong" way to meditate. Let the pages serve you and be open to the emotions and thoughts that arise within you for each.

RISE

mini mindful morning meditations

"The little things?
The little moments?
They aren't little."

– Jon Kabat-Zinn

LITTLE THINGS

begin to slow your breathing
listen to the sound of each inhale and exhale
allow each breath to fill you with droplets of gratitude

starting with the soles of your feet
slowly moving to the crown of your head
guide your breath into every cell of your body

as your breath flows for you
in and out
repeat the words to yourself
"thank you"

when you feel ready
close your eyes
and answer this question in your mind

what are the little things you are grateful for today?

allow the answers to float to the surface of your mind
acknowledge them
send them gratitude
and then let them drift away

place your hands on your heart
and once again
fill this moment and your day ahead
with gratitude
by simply repeating the words
"thank you"

"For fast acting relief,
try slowing down."

– Lily Tomlin

ZEN IN TEN

with each deep inhale
one at a time
slowly say these words in your mind

release

reset

calm

quiet

soft

peaceful

tranquil

harmony

compassion

love

repeat...and embody the feelings
that each word brings to you

"You can search throughout the entire universe for someone who is more deserving of your love and affection than you are yourself, and that person is not to be found anywhere. You, yourself, as much as anybody in the entire universe, deserve your love and affection."

– Sharon Salzberg

MORNING METTA

*Metta is an ancient
Buddhist meditation
practice for cultivating
feelings of love and kindness.*

take a few long
slow and deep
breaths

close your eyes
see yourself in your mind
almost as if you are
outside looking in

as you connect to
your essence
direct these words to you
with love and kindness
in your heart

MAY YOU BE SAFE
MAY YOU BE HEALTHY
MAY YOU BE HAPPY
MAY YOU BE LOVED

*shift your awareness
to another*
someone you care

deeply about
as you see them
in your mind
and connect to
their essence
direct these words
to them

MAY YOU BE SAFE
MAY YOU BE HEALTHY
MAY YOU BE HAPPY
MAY YOU BE LOVED

now hold the entire
world in your mind
every creature, animal,
element, and soul
as you see it all in
front of you
and connect to the
essence of the universe
direct these words to it all

MAY YOU BE SAFE
MAY YOU BE HEALTHY
MAY YOU BE HAPPY
MAY YOU BE LOVED

"There are no rules.
Just follow your heart."

– Robin Williams

CLARITY

before you begin
ask yourself this question

what is an answer i currently seek?

place your hands over your heart
slow your breathing
feel your thoughts calming
your body relaxing
your heart beating for you

with your eyes closed
complete these statements below in your mind
one at a time
allow the answers to flow through you

in regards to this situation, my mind is saying _____

in regards to this situation, my body is saying _____

in regards to this situation, my heart is saying _____

throughout the day
connect with your mind + body + heart for clarity
they each have unique guidance to offer you

"In meditation you take an unbiased approach.
You let things be as they are, without judgment,
and in that way you yourself learn to be."

– Pema Chödrön

MINDFUL BEGINNING

find a quiet place to be

witness what you are feeling

notice the thoughts you are having

become aware of the sensations that you are
experiencing

be gentle with yourself

place no judgment

to just be

right here

right now

is enough

"I have met myself and I am going to
take care of [me] fiercely."

– Glennon Doyle

HEALING BODY SCAN

get cozy
sitting up or lying down
whatever you prefer

take deep inhales
drawing healing breath
into your body

releasing any discomfort
through audible exhales

move your awareness
slowly into each part of
your body
beginning with the soles
of your feet
moving to your ankles
your calves
knees
thighs
breathe into your pelvis
lower back
your abdomen
up your spine
fill your lungs

let it out
breathe into your heart
feel your chest rise and
fall
breath into your
shoulders
throat
relax your jaw
your entire face
breathe into your third
eye
allow it to feel a rush of
light
breathe all the way to the
top of your head

anywhere you are holding
tension
release it, let it go

stay here
just breathing
inviting and welcoming
healing

"There is always light. If only we're brave enough
to see it. If only we're brave enough to be it."

– Amanda Gorman

WAKING INTENTION

sit in a quiet place
begin to gradually look around you
take in what surrounds you

as you settle in and feel centered
answer these questions

what are 5 objects you notice around you?

4 colors that stand out?

3 sounds that you hear?

2 sensations that you feel?

now close your eyes as you answer this final question

what is 1 intention you would like to set for today?

"Live in the present, launch yourself on every wave, find eternity in each moment."

– Henry David Thoreau

MOMENT MAKING

slow your breathing
listen to your inhales
and exhales
take your time
be in this moment

when you feel present
answer these questions
in your mind

*WHO is someone that you
are looking forward to
spending time with today?*

close your eyes and see
them in your mind
notice their qualities
and characteristics
feel their energy
with yours
be in the moment that
you are with them
hold it in your mind
and send that precious
time your gratitude

*WHAT is a situation that
you are looking forward to
being present for today?*

visualize this moment
happening right now

see yourself there
fill your mind with the
details of its occurrence
be present within it
and send it your gratitude

*WHERE is a place that you
are looking forward to being
present within today?*

see the details of
the setting
where are you
what sounds do you hear
what feelings do you
have when you are there
put yourself in the place
and send it your gratitude

*WHEN is a particular
moment that you are
looking forward to being
present within today?*

imaging that moment
allow time to slow down
submerse yourself in it
feel it
just be there
and once again
send it your gratitude

"We become what we think about. Energy flows where attention goes."

– Rhonda Byrne

MORNING MANIFESTATION

what is something that you
deeply desire for yourself?

a dream
a goal
an experience
an adventure
a connection

place no limit on
your desire

close your eyes
see it happening for you
right now
in this moment

layer your vision
with detail

where are you?

what do you see?

what colors are around you?

what do you smell?

what sounds do you hear?

what are you feeling
internally and externally?

who are you with?

what is happening for you?

align your energy with
every aspect of what you
are visualizing for yourself

become it by embodying it

carry this energy with
you throughout the day

and if the vision gets lost
come back to meditation
close your eyes
and see it happening
for you once again

"So let the mind flow like water. Face life with a calm and quiet mind and everything in life will be calm and quiet."

– Thich Thien-An

SUNKISSED

see yourself sitting next to the sea
feel the sand on your toes
a light breeze upon your face
notice the smell of salty air
warmth pouring onto your sunkissed skin

use your breath to calm your mind and your body
let your inhales and exhales
move like a flowing dance
just like the waves

roll in
roll out
let it in
let it out

roll in
roll out
let it in
let it out

roll in
roll out
let it in
let it out

"If you change the way you look at things,
the things around you often change."

– Dr. Wayne Dyer

MAGIC EYES

look all around you
really look
notice the way light lands
how it creates shadows
layers of brightness and darkness

close your eyes
invite magic within
by repeating this affirmation

today, i will see everything through magic in my eyes

after a few minutes
open your eyes

see everything new again
the light
the shadows
the layers of brightness and darkness

and once again repeat

today, i will see everything through magic in my eyes

"We are what we think. All that we are arises with our thoughts. With our thoughts, we make the world."

– The Buddha

SPARK JOY

calm your mind and body
by following this cyclical breathing rhythm

inhale through your nose to the count of 1..2..3..4
pause at the top and hold your breath for 1..2..3..4
exhale through your mouth to the count of 1..2..3..4
pause at the bottom and hold your breath for 1..2..3..4

repeat until you feel your senses relax

when you are ready
close your eyes and
answer this question in your mind

what brings you joy?

invite the images of moments
faces
places
activities
memories
that make you smile
that light you up on the inside
that spark joy
to come to mind

celebrate each as they come to you
let them fill you with feelings of happiness
embody this joy
and try to carry it with you throughout your day

"Life is a balance of holding on and letting go."

– Rumi

MAKE IT RIGHT

*This meditation is the healing Hawaiian practice
of Ho'oponopono, which means to "make it
right". These words bring balance into life.*

repeat in your mind each of the words below
simply saying them is enough to
create healing and balance

direct them to yourself
to others
towards anything or anyone that comes up for you
without judgment
with grace and kindness
releasing the emotions that may come with them

I'M SORRY

PLEASE FORGIVE ME

THANK YOU

I LOVE YOU

"Talk to yourself like someone you love."

– Brené Brown

SELF-LOVIN' MANTRAS

sit up tall for this meditation
slightly roll your shoulders back
gently lift your chin

visualize yourself in your favorite place
a place you love to be
where you feel completely at ease

when you feel yourself there
repeat these chakra-healing mantras:

I am grounded, connected and rooted in my body

I am compassionate with myself and
I allow my feelings to flow

I am protective of my inner light

I am open to giving and receiving unconditional love

I am authentically expressive with my voice

I am guided by my powerful intuition

I am a part of everything and everything is a part of me

"Feelings come and go like clouds in a windy sky. Conscious breathing is my anchor."

– Thich Nhat Hanh

AWAKENING BREATH

before your eyes even open in the morning
listen to the sound of your breath
inhale slowly through your nose
exhale audibly through your mouth

turn your breath into a conscious rhythm
inhale 1..2..3..4..5
exhale 1..2..3..4..5

listen to the life that each breath brings to you
place your hands on your heart
feel it beating for you

each breath
a new beginning
gradually awakening you to this beautiful morning

"Do you press the "pause" button – the "until" button in life by saying "I can't be happy until..."? Press the "play" button and rejoice in the nowness of the moment."

– Michael Bernard Beckwith

BE HERE NOW

today
right now
this moment
is happening *for* you

life
it is happening
through you

take this moment
to notice the blocks
within your thoughts
your actions
your perceptions

release them
let them fly away

take this moment
to welcome
a new openness
a new beginning
a fresh start
for your thoughts
your actions
your perceptions

today, and every day, you are exactly
where you are supposed to be

"The things that make me different
are the things that make me."

– *Winnie the Pooh*, A.A. Milne

YOU.

there is no one like you
in this entire world

the unique way that you see things
the way that you pour your heart into what you love
the way you talk
what makes you laugh
how you cry
the way you dance

take this time to reflect on how
incredibly special it is to be YOU

thank you for being you

"Live in the sunshine, swim in the sea, drink the wild air."

– Ralph Waldo Emerson

SUNRISE

sweet sunlight
rising above the sea
as far as my eye can see

soak up my body
envelop my soul
warm me from the outside in

and for today
may I give back
ALL
of the warmth
the comfort
the healing
that you have just given to me

(repeat)

"When I let go of what I am, I become what I might be."

– Lao Tzu

MORNING RAIN

close your eyes

feel a storm coming in the distance

hear the rain beginning to fall around you

feel the drops upon your skin

let the water melt away any worries

washing away stress

freeing you of tension

clearing your mind

opening your heart

creating for you a new beginning

to make today whatever you want it to be

to become whoever you want to be

"Walk as if you are kissing the ground with your feet."

– Thich Nhat Hanh

WANDER WALKING

*if standing is not available,
it is perfectly aligned
to do this meditation
in your mind*

stand up very gently

place your feet firmly on
the ground beneath you

take 3 slow breaths

feel your chest rise and
fall with each breath

connect to the sensations
within your body

slowly, slowly, slowly

begin to lift one foot
off the ground

place it in front of you

roll your foot from
your heal to your toes

as your body guides you

into a forward motion

take another step

and another, and another

as you slowly move
around your space

be fully present
in the motion

feeling everything
within your body

and when you are ready

be still

place a hand on your
heart and a hand on
your abdomen

say these words to
yourself and to your body

*THANK YOU
THANK YOU
THANK YOU*

"Emancipate yourselves from mental slavery,
none but ourselves can free our minds."

– Bob Marley

MINDSET FREEDOM

when you let go
of that which is
not serving you
you create space
for new

prepare for this
meditation
by gently slowing
your breath
opening your heart
and
giving yourself permission
to let go

when you feel open
to letting go
meditate upon
these questions
giving yourself space
between each

*what thoughts are you
ready to release?*

*what is your body
ready to let go of?*

*what within your heart
is ready to be set free?*

now that you
have released
you have created freedom
in your mind
body
heart

answer these questions

*what new mindset are
you ready to embody?*

*what new actions are
you ready to take that
support your body?*

*what are you ready to
cultivate within your heart?*

"The universe operates through dynamic exchange...
giving and receiving are different aspects of
the flow of energy in the universe... and in our
willingness to give that which we seek, we keep the
abundance of the universe circulating in our lives."

– Deepak Chopra

ABUNDANCE

what is the abundance
that you seek and desire
right now, in *this*
moment?

is it love
money
kindness
health
experience
forgiveness

anything you want...say
out loud what you want

CLAIM IT

now, with your eyes closed

visualize yourself *giving* it

this exact same thing
that which you so
deeply desire

see yourself giving
it to someone else

see them in your mind

see the moment that
you give this to them

witness them receiving it

*how does it feel for
you, to give?*

embody the feelings
of giving
to align your energy
with its positivity

this is the law of
giving and receiving
activate it by first giving
that which you desire
and the Universe will
reward you tenfold

"You have been criticizing yourself for years.
Try approving of yourself and see what happens."

– Louise Haye

FRESH START

slowly inhale to the
count of 1..2..3..4
hold your breath 1..2
exhale 1..2..3..4
hold your breath 1..2

continue this breathwork
with your awareness
only on your breath
until you feel an
inner shift

allow your breath to
return to its normal
cadence, and as you do...

inhale FREE

exhale JUDGMENT

inhale TRUST

exhale FEAR

inhale PEACE

exhale ANGER

inhale ABUNDANCE

exhale SCARCITY

inhale HEALTH

exhale PAIN

inhale SURRENDER

exhale STRESS

and now

inhale and exhale
LOVE for yourself

inhale and exhale
LOVE for others

inhale and exhale
LOVE for today

you have just created
a fresh start

have a beautiful day

"It was when I stopped searching for home within others
and lifted the foundations of home within myself I
found there were no roots more intimate than those
between a mind and body that have decided to be whole."

– Rupi Kaur

GROUNDED

place your feet firmly on the ground in front of you
sit up as straight as possible

imagine yourself surrounded by nature
in the midst of a vibrantly green jungle
with your bare feet on the ground
touching the rich soil beneath you

feel the energy of the earth
surging into you
supporting you
grounding you

repeat these affirmations in your mind

I am grounded

I am rooted

I am connected

I am whole

"Breathe quietly and let it be. Let your body relax and your heart soften."

– Jack Kornfield

SPACE AND GRACE

every moment
in life
brings an opportunity
to open *more*
to experience *more*
to love *more*

try and breathe softly
sweetly
to let yourself just be

close your eyes
and gift yourself
the space and grace
to fill this moment
your mind
your body
your heart
your entire being
with *more*
of what you need
more of what brings you peace and happiness

"Inner darkness, which we call ignorance, is the root of suffering. The more inner light that comes, the more darkness will diminish. This is the only way to achieve salvation or nirvana."

– Dalai Lama

INNER SUNSHINE

close your eyes
visualize yourself outside
on a day filled with sunshine
feel the warmth of the sunlight upon your skin
surrounding you in light

rub your hand together
to create warmth and energy flowing through you
place your hands upon your upper abdomen
your solar plexus
your center of light
your inner sunshine

let your breath fill this space
drawing sunlight from the outside in
feel your abdomen rising and falling
each breath igniting your inner light

repeat this mantra in your mind
over...and over...and over

I AM LIGHT

"If you are distressed by anything external, the pain is not due to the thing itself but to your own estimate of it; and this you have the power to revoke at any moment."

– Marcus Aurelius

STRESSOLUTION

lie down and close your eyes

inhale through your nose
focus on the numbers
and count in your mind 1..2..3

exhale through your mouth
again, focusing on the numbers
and count in your mind 1..2..3

if your thoughts wander
come back to the counting
and listen to your breath

practice this breathing for a few minutes
resetting your parasympathetic nervous system
allowing stress to melt away

"When you awaken love and laughter in your life, your mind lets go of fear and anxiety, and your happy spirit becomes the healing balm that transforms every aspect of your human experience."

– Jesse Dylan

DAYLIGHT DELIGHT

kick up your legs
throw it back
get really really really comfortable

can you laugh at today
before it barely begins
try it
belly laugh
no judgment
from the deepest parts of your being

let it all out
and just laugh
and laugh
and laugh

let this moment be silly and perfect
just as it is

"Be the flow."

– Jay-Z

FLOW

everything that is not meant for you
is ready for you to release it

open your mind and heart
allow it to float away

let it go

everything that is meant for you
is ready to come your way

open your mind and heart
welcome it your way

let it in

everything that you need to know
is ready to reveal itself

open your mind and heart
it is already inside of you

let it flow

"My growth is entwined with my positive state of mind."

– Jennifer Williamson

I AM

7 morning I AM affirmations to repeat as you wake up

today...

I AM going to be loving to myself

I AM going to be gentle with my thoughts

I AM going to nourish my body

I AM holding forgiveness in my heart

I AM kind with my voice

I AM present with my actions

I AM me, and that is enough

"I will not let anyone walk through my
mind with their dirty feet."

– Mahatma Gandhi

SELF-PROTECTION

visualize a circle of white protective
light surrounding you

this light is safe
warm
comforting
nurturing

this light is protecting you from all
external negative energy

only those that you invite in
those who lift you higher
are welcome into it

for a few minutes
get clarity on who you want to
share your light with today

this could be just you

a select few

or whoever comes to mind
whatever is right for you
allow mediation to guide your way

before leaving this meditation
repeat in your mind
an affirmation for today

love is the only entry point

"You will find that it is necessary to let things go;
simply for the reason that they are heavy. So let them
go, let go of them. I tie no weights to my ankles."

– C. JoyBell C.

LETTING GO

*To consciously let go of the
thoughts, energetic cords,
and actions that no longer
serve and support you
is vital to the regeneration
of your life, health
and happiness.*

as you begin to take
deep breaths
repeat in your mind

*i am willing to let go
i welcome this release*

when you are ready...
imagine yourself sitting
next to a body of water
the ocean, a river, a lake
whatever you
like the most

as you take in the beauty
that surrounds you
visualize yourself
picking up a stone
hold it and feel it
in your hand
fill it with the intention
of what you are letting go

*as you set this intention
say out loud to yourself
what you are releasing*

*i am willing and ready
to let go of _____*

see yourself throwing this
stone into the water
and as you do, repeat
the phrase i am
letting you go

repeat this releasing
process
stone after stone
until you feel that you
have let go of everything
that is not serving you

when you are ready
come back into this
present moment
celebrate the space
you have just created
for yourself
by no longer carrying
that which is ready to go

"Your greatest power is to show love, to
receive love and to be love."

– Oprah Winfrey

LOVE EMBODIMENT

love
sweet
love

is there ever
really
a
more clear choice
but to be open
to giving
receiving
and being
unconditional love?

take a few minutes
to mindfully inhale
and exhale
drawing love into
your body

when you are ready
answer these questions
in your mind

how do you like to give love?

*how do you like to
receive love?*

how do you like to be love?

throughout this day
let the love you have just
created flow through
your entire being
every drop of it
give it
receive it
embody it

"Apparently there is nothing that cannot happen today."

– Mark Twain

ADVENTURE MINDSET

visualize yourself
standing at the beginning
of a long hallway
at the other end
is a large mysterious door

the adventure that awaits
on the other side
is *entirely* up to you

see yourself walking
slowly towards the door

1st step
everything before this
moment is left behind you

2nd step
your body feels as ease

3rd step
you feel a spark of
excitement ignite
within you

4th step
a new energy is
beginning to rise

5th step

a slight smile spreads
across your face

6th step
a childlike curiosity is
drawing you closer

7th step
your imagination
is opening

8th step
see your hand slowly
reach out in front of you
opening the door

*what do you see on
the other side?*

*what adventure
lies before you?*

*walk into the space and let
your imagination run wild...*

spend as much time
here as you would like
put no limit on the
adventure you are able
to create for yourself

"Thoughts come and go. Feelings come and go. Find out what it is that remains."

– Ramana Maharshi

SIGNS

are you open to the signs?

the signs within you and around you
guiding your way

who would you like a sign from?

what do you need guidance on?

close your eyes

ask for signs
be specific in your request

open your eyes
go out into the world
and be open to the signs
within you
all around you
that are guiding and supporting your path

"This is a wonderful day, I have
never seen this one before."

– Maya Angelou

SOUL FOOD

what feeds your soul?

close your eyes
envision it all

soft blankets
belly laughs
your favorite meal

hugs from friends
deep talks
a warm bath

a good book
music to sing to
a poem to cry to

what is it for you...
that which makes your soul sing?

"Creativity is inventing, experimenting, growing, taking risks, breaking rules, making mistakes, and having fun."

– Mary Lou Cook

UNLEASH CREATIVITY

use this meditation
to tap into your inner child
and *unleash* your creative energy

take some deep breaths
release control
release time
release judgment
let go of everything on the outside world

close your eyes
and find the silly side inside
the part that makes you smile
the part of you that is always ready to have fun

now *let loose*

turn on music if you would like
move your body
get awkward with it
let yourself jump, twist, turn, flow, dance
whatever your body feels like doing
move freely
let your wild
inner child
be the guide

"You wanna fly, you got to give up the
sh*t that weighs you down."

– Toni Morrison

FLOATING

lie down and get
comfortable
for a moment feel
everything

the surface you
are lying on
the way your clothes
touch your skin
how your body rises and
falls with each breath
any pressure or
feelings you are
holding onto within

close your eyes
imagine that you
are standing on the
edge of a river
a river that flows gently
calling to you
to come and float within it

see yourself slowly taking
steps into the warm river
1..2..3

with each inhale feel the

water rising up your body
4..5..6

imagine yourself
swimming
and turning onto
your back
7..8..9

floating with ease
10

feel the water move
around your body
removing any tension
releasing any feelings
soothing your
mind and body

stay here

floating and breathing
allowing the water
to wash away
anything weighing
you down
be free

"What keeps life fascinating is the constant creativity of the soul."

– Deepak Chopra

IGNITE ENERGY

the soul is the part of you that has boundless energy

there are times when
our minds run in circles
our bodies get tired

but *not* the soul

the soul holds and eternal energetic supply of vitality
ready for you to tap into
anytime you would like

to activate this energy
practice infinity breath for 5 minutes

to do so...
visualize an infinity sign in your mind
as you follow the path of the sign
inhale for the first half of the sign
exhale for second half of the sign
creating a dynamic flow of equal breathing

as your soul energy becomes engaged
allow your breath to return to its normal flow
and fill your mind and body with this new
flowing source of boundless energy

"And, when you want something, all the universe conspires in helping you to achieve it."

– Paulo Coelho

PAINT YOUR DAY

as the sun is rising
your day beginning
become the painter
of today's blank canvas

close your eyes and reflect on this
important question in your mind

what do you want to create for yourself today?

see the beautiful moments in your mind
hold them
feel them
experience them
as if they are happening for you now

and remember to be present with them
as they unfold
throughout the day

"The more light you allow within you the brighter the world you live in will be."

– Shakti Gawain

TURN THE LIGHTS DOWN LOW

shut the shades
close the outside light
this time is for you

see an inner light within you
growing brighter with each breath

take some time to reflect on the following questions

what will spark your inner light today?

how do you want to protect your inner light today?

how do you want to shine your inner light today?

your light is uniquely yours
it is yours to shine or to keep to yourself
it is yours to attract what you desire
or to turn away what you do not

use your inner light to recognize what makes you shine

"There is a voice that doesn't use words. Listen."

– Rumi.

INTUITION

your intuition thrives within your third eye
your center of deeper knowing

let's ignite it...

close your eyes
visualize a bright violet light
beaming into your third eye
the space between your brows
see this light opening your intuition

after a few minutes

use your intuition to gain clarity in 3 areas of life...

think about a decision you would like clarity on

what is your intuition telling you?

think about a relationship you would like clarity on

what is your intuition telling you?

think about an opportunity you would like clairty on

what is your intuition telling you?

throughout the day
allow your intuition to guide you

with your trust
it will not steer you wrong

"Beauty begins the moment you decide to be yourself."

– Coco Chanel

AUTHENTIC VOICE

your voice
how your communicate
how you authentically express yourself
is divinely unique to you

the tone you use
the cadence
the strength and power of your voice
the purpose of your words
are always yours to choose

bring awareness into your throat
tap it gently 3 times
with each breath visualize a beautiful blue
light opening and freeing your voice

as this light does its healing work
reflect on this question

how will I use my authentic voice today?

for the rest of the day
and every day
be you

"Everything amazing about the universe is inside of you, and the two are inseparable."

– Carl Sagan

STARDUST

imagine yourself underneath a sky full of stars

see the lights twinkling
galaxies
constellations
planets
dancing all around you

feel your body
your bones
muscles
skin

your body is made of 93% stardust

which means *you* are a part of the sky full of stars

"Paradise is to love many things with a passion."

– Pablo Picasso

GLOW

Tummo is an ancient meditation practiced by Tibetan Buddhist Monks. With Tummo breath and visualization you are able to burn away negative thoughts and simultaneously heat up your body which lowers blood pressure, cleanses your heart and lungs, clears your mind, and lights an inner fire.

Here are the steps:

sit in an upright position with your
hands resting on your stomach

close your eyes and focus on relaxing and clearing
your mind of negative thoughts the best that you can

visualize a flame lit within your stomach

as you inhale through your nose,
slightly arch your back

allow the fire to rise up your spine with your breath
as you exhale through your mouth,
round your spine inward
allowing the flames to retreat back to your stomach
continue this breath for 8-10 rounds
feel a heat rise within you
burning away negativity
cleansing your mind & body
lighting your inner flame

"Every success story is a tale of constant adaptation, revision and change."

– Richard Branson

TRANSFORMATION

*This meditation is to open
your mind, body, and
heart to transformation.
A gentle reminder that
life is happening for you
and through you, always.*

let's connect and go in...

slow down
and
breathe deeply

your thoughts solely
focused on the sound
of your breath

when you feel calm and
connected, answer these
questions in your mind

*is your mindset open
to transformation?*

*are you physically open
to transformation?*

*are you emotionally open
to transformation?*

repeat these phrases
to release

*in this moment, i
release all fear*

*in this moment, i
release all self-doubt*

*in this moment, i
release control*

repeat these mantras
to transform

*in this moment, i
will surrender*

in this moment, i will trust

*in this moment, i am
transforming*

"Because in the end, you won't remember the times you spent in the office or mowing the lawn. Climb the goddamn mountain."

– Jack Karouac

SOUL PLAY

soak up the feelings these words stir within you

wander

adventure

curious

wild

spontaneous

awestruck

serendipitous

magical

meaningful

destined

what experience does your soul want to have today?

grant yourself permission to play

let your soul lead the way

"What comes, when it comes, will be what it is."

– Alberto Caeiro

SWEET SERENITY

the definition of serenity:
the state of being calm, peaceful, and untroubled

what if, for the next few minutes

you choose to simply surrender and trust?

"The question isn't about who is going to let me; it's who is going to stop me."

– Ayn Rand

LIMITLESS

your crown chakra
at the very top of your head
is the energy center that connects you
to everything within you
and everything around you

when your crown is open
you are limitless

close your eyes
visualize yourself outside
the sunlight upon your face
allow your body to relax
put your mind to ease

feel the sunlight beam into the top of your head
healing and gently opening your crown chakra

as you welcome this light
repeat these phrases

today has infinite possibilities

i am open to receiving all of the light that is coming my way

there is no limit to what i am able to create for myself

"Greatness comes by doing a few small and smart things each and every day. Comes from taking little steps, consistently. Comes from making a few small chips against everything in your professional and personal life that is ordinary, so that a day eventually arrives when all that's left is The Extraordinary."

– Robin S. Sharma

EXTRAORDINARY

Are you open to the extraordinary that today will bring?

sit quietly
recognize
feel
embrace
how extraordinary *this* very moment is

to *just be* is an extraordinary miracle

when you feel ready

set the motion of the day into action
by repeating to yourself

something EXTRAORDINARY is going to happen today
i don't know when
i don't know where
i don't know how
but i can't wait to find out

QUOTES INCLUDED IN RISE

"The little things? The little moments?
They aren't little." – Jon Kabat-Zinn

"For fast acting relief, try slowing down." – Lily Tomlin

"You can search throughout the entire universe for
someone who is more deserving of your love and
affection than you are yourself, and that person
is not to be found anywhere. You, yourself, as
much as anybody in the entire universe, deserve
your love and affection." – Sharon Salzberg

"There are no rules. Just follow
your heart." – Robin Williams

"In meditation you take an unbiased approach. You
let things be as they are, without judgment, and in
that way you yourself learn to be." – Pema Chödrön

"I have met myself and I am going to take
care of [me] fiercely" – Glennon Doyle

"There is always light. If only we're brave
enough to see it. If only we're brave
enough to be it." – Amanda Gorman

"Live in the present, launch yourself on every wave, find
eternity in each moment." – Henry David Thoreau

"We become what we think about. Energy flows
where attention goes." – Rhonda Byrne

"So let the mind flow like water. Face life with a calm and quiet mind and everything in life will be calm and quiet." – Thich Thien-An

"If you change the way you look at things, the things around you often change." – Dr. Wayne Dyer

"We are what we think. All that we are arises with our thoughts. With our thoughts, we make the world." – The Buddha

"Life is a balance of holding on and letting go." – Rumi

"Talk to yourself like someone you love." – Brené Brown

"Feelings come and go like clouds in a windy sky. Conscious breathing is my anchor." – Thich Nhat Hanh

"Do you press the "pause" button – the "until" button in life by saying "I can't be happy until…"? Press the "play" button and rejoice in the nowness of the moment." – Michael Bernard Beckwith

"The things that make me different are the things that make me." – *Winnie the Pooh*, A.A. Milne

"Live in the sunshine, swim the sea, drink the wild air." – Ralph Waldo Emerson

"When I let go of what I am, I become what I might be." – Lao Tzu

"Walk as if you are kissing the ground with your feet." – Thich Nhat Hanh

"Emancipate yourselves from mental slavery, none but ourselves can free our minds." – Bob Marley

"The universe operates through dynamic exchange... giving and receiving are different aspects of the flow of energy in the universe... and in our willingness to give that which we seek, we keep the abundance of the universe circulating in our lives." – Deepak Chopra

"You have been criticizing yourself for years. Try approving of yourself and see what happens." – Louise Haye

"It was when I stopped searching for home within others and lifted the foundations of home within myself I found there were no roots more intimate than those between a mind and body that have decided to be whole." – Rupi Kaur

"Breathe quietly and let it be. Let your body relax and your heart soften." – Jack Kornfield

"Inner darkness, which we call ignorance, is the root of suffering. The more inner light that comes, the more darkness will diminish. This is the only way to achieve salvation or nirvana.." – Dalai Lama

"If you are distressed by anything external, the pain is not due to the thing itself but to your own estimate of it; and this you have the power to revoke at any moment." – Marcus Aurelius

"When you awaken love and laughter in your life, your mind lets go of fear and anxiety, and your happy spirit becomes the healing balm that transforms every aspect of your human experience." – Jesse Dylan

"Be the flow." – Jay-Z

"My growth is entwined with my positive
state of mind." – Jennifer Williamson

"I will not let anyone walk through my mind
with their dirty feet." – Mahatma Gandhi

"You will find that it is necessary to let things go; simply
for the reason that they are heavy. So let them go, let go
of them. I tie no weights to my ankles." – C. JoyBell C.

"Your greatest power is to show love, to receive
love and to be love." – Oprah Winfrey

"Apparently there is nothing that cannot
happen today." – Mark Twain

"Thoughts come and go. Feelings come and go. Find
out what it is that remains." – Ramana Maharshi

"This is a wonderful day, I have never seen
this one before." – Maya Angelou

"Creativity is inventing, experimenting,
growing, taking risks, breaking rules, making
mistakes, and having fun." – Mary Lou Cook

"You wanna fly, you got to give up the sh*t
that weighs you down." – Toni Morrison

"What keeps life fascinating is the constant
creativity of the soul." – Deepak Chopra

"And, when you want something, all the universe
conspires in helping you to achieve it." – Paulo Coelho

"The more light you allow within you the brighter
the world you live in will be." – Shakti Gawain

"There is a voice that doesn't use words. Listen." – Rumi

"Beauty begins the moment you decide
to be yourself." – Coco Chanel

"Everything amazing about the universe is inside of
you, and the two are inseparable." – Carl Sagan

"Paradise is to love many things with
a passion." – Pablo Picasso

"Every success story is a tale of constant adaptation,
revision and change." – Richard Branson

"Because in the end, you won't remember the times
you spent in the office or mowing the lawn. Climb
the goddamn mountain." – Jack Karouac

"What comes, when it comes, will be
what it is." – Alberto Caeiro

"The question isn't about who is going to let me;
it's who is going to stop me." – Ayn Rand

"Greatness comes by doing a few small and smart
things each and every day. Comes from taking
little steps, consistently. Comes from making
a few small chips against everything in your
professional and personal life that is ordinary,
so that a day eventually arrives when all that's
left is The Extraordinary." – Robin S. Sharma

ABOUT THE AUTHOR

Julie Skon is a multi-modality healing practitioner based in Los Angeles, California. She is a life & trauma healing coach, a global meditation teacher featured on Insight Timer & The Head Plan, an IIN integrative nutrition health coach, Reiki Master, author, and is wildly passionate about discovering and sharing methods to grow, heal, and thrive.

To listen to these meditations and experience them LIVE with Julie or for coaching inquiries, visit her website www.myrituelle.com or follow her on instagram @julieskon.

Julie would LOVE to hear about your experience with the meditations in RISE. Please contact her at julie@myrituelle.com.

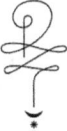